The Light Within
Copyright © 2016 Stephanie Henry

Published by: Bookbaby, Pennsauken NJ, USA, 2016.

ISBN 978-1-48357-186-7

For the bright ones and those in need of light: whichever you are, whenever you are.

There is a brilliant flame inside of you, but it takes special care to see it shine through.

Close your eyes and let your mind
be free. Use your imagination to see.

Behind your ribs, deep within your heart,
beats a flame with endless light to impart.

Your flame carries the happiness
you feel inside. It comes from
within but can spread far and wide.

It brightens your day when you're
feeling down; reminds you to smile,
rather than frown.

Look to your flame for thoughts you hold dear, giving you hope and casting away fear.

Just as you hold a candle close when you walk, shield your flame so winds will be blocked.

When others are feeling sad, angry or blue, they'll see a bright light when they look at you.

They might use your flame to brighten
their own, making yours feel dim
and blown.

Others could blow out your flame and scamper away, leaving you in a cold shade of grey.

When things don't seem to be going your way, it can lead to a gloomy, dim day.

You'll be left feeling down, stirring about, sitting inside a shadow of doubt.

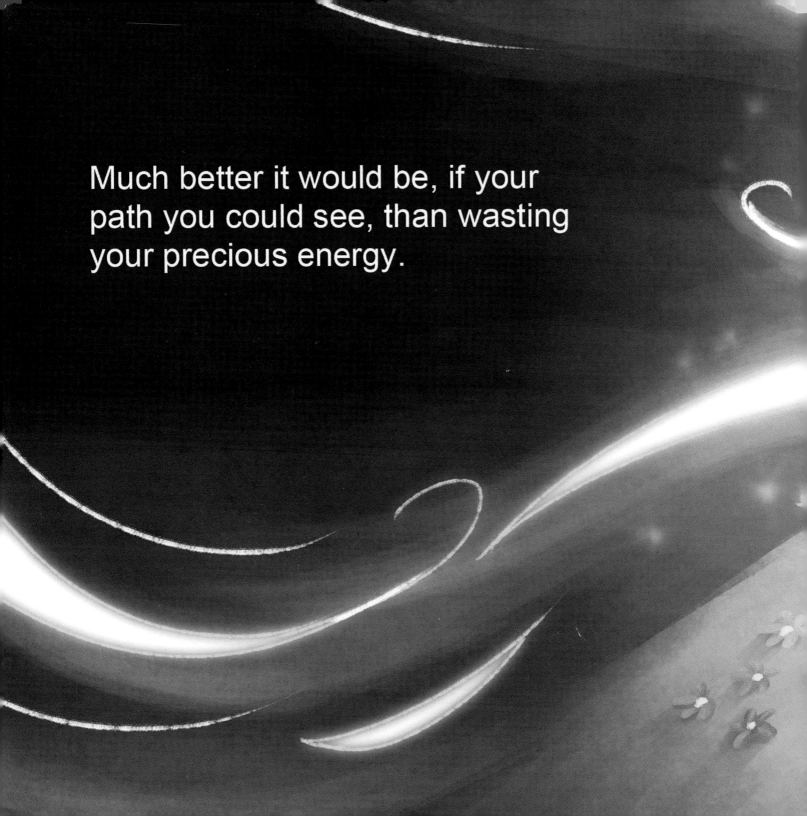

Much better it would be, if your path you could see, than wasting your precious energy.

It's much easier to light a candle than stay in the dark, so dig deep within and find that dazzling spark.

Imagine things to be grateful for, things to delight, and all that darkness will turn into light.

With practice, you'll spot flame-blowers from afar. It's no fault of yours for the way they are.

Just know others have stories
untold. They need a special
love when their flame turns cold.

Surely they don't aim to be hurtful
or mean. Lend them your light,
for they're battling something
unseen.

Like kindness, when given, flame multiplies.
Let yours reach the highest of skies.

Share the light, from one candle to another.
Be the spark that ignites every other.

A flame doesn't cease from lighting another.
Instead, spreading from one to the other,
to the other.

Lighting one flame quickly turns into three: an infinite state of turning me into we.

That's the beauty of a flame – it's brighter when shared; brilliant on its own but better when paired.

With dimness inside, there's little to give. You must kindle your flame for as long as you live.

It'll burn strong when you're feeling well, so reach for thoughts that happiness tells.

A unicorn prancing, writing songs
in the sky. A soft little puppy,
chasing a butterfly.

Imagine all things that make your
heart sing. Take time to relish
the gifts life brings.

Surround yourself with bright people and things that glow. Keep a flame full of happiness wherever you go.

The way you feel is all up to you:
it starts with your thoughts and
reflects in all you do.

Take a moment to choose and
things will align. The feeling you
pick is the one that will shine.

Will you choose to be happy?
Or choose to be mad? Make others
feel good? Or make them feel bad?

Each moment brings a gift of happiness,
when you choose to spread
light and kindness.

Life's winds or darkness may one day come to pass, but the dimness inside doesn't need to last.

Though there may come a time
when you feel blue, it is then to
yourself you must always be true.

Look to your flame to help
see you through: those magical
thoughts that lie within you.

Whatever you look for is what
you will see…
And the brighter you are, the
brighter you will be.

For free resources to use at home
or in the classroom, please visit
www.stephaniehenrybooks.com